BIPOLAR LEXICON
An Akathisia of Expressed Emotion

Poems by
Megan Denese Mealor

Published by Unsolicited Press
www.unsolicitedpress.com
info@unsolicitedpress.com

Copyright © 2018 Megan Denese Mealor
All Rights Reserved.

No part of this book may be reproduced or transmitted in any form or by any means without written permission from the publisher or author.

Unsolicited Press Books are distributed by Ingram.
Printed in the United States of America.

Attention schools and businesses: for discounted copies on large orders, please contact the publisher directly.

Cover Art: Marnie Villenueva
Editor: S.R. Stewart

ISBN: 978-1-947021-47-1

BIPOLAR LEXICON
An Akathisia of Expressed Emotion

*"In the end, she became more than what she expected.
She became the journey, and like all journeys, she did not end;
she just simply changed directions and kept going."*

-R.M. Drake

Contents

Without Poetry	1
Ripening	2
freshman girl	3
Little Punk	4
listening for it . . .	5
Color-Coded & Iridescent	6
Softer	7
Vilano	8
Tide	9
Adulterer	10
Bipolar Lexicon	11
Addictions	12
Distance	13
Obstinance	14
Waif	15
Psych Ward, Fifth Floor	17
a ravaged statue	18
Grown into the Atmosphere	19
Hermit	20
A Faith, Rotting	21
the darkest art	22
To Whomever Listens Here	24
deployed	25
A Single History	26
Mischief	27
mockings, midnights	28
Relics	31
White Light	33
Interstate, Idle	34
Ode to Anonymous Annulment	35
Whitechapel	36

Suicide Attack	37
Cave Art	38
Pappaw	39
A Distant Relation	41
Asylum Patient 141	42
Wednesday Night on the Ward	44
Now Lucid	46
Farewell to Seafaring	48
Green River Eulogy	49
Five Mornings Later	50
Brothers	51
The Ones Before Ours	53
Mapping	54
Acknowledgments	55
About the Author	59
About the Press	60

*For my gentle-hearted father,
who held my hand
in darkened times
and read to me
when silences became burdens.*

*And for my lion-willed mother,
composed of gumption, grit, and gold,
whose story knows no bounds.*

Without Poetry

we are delusions
we are vipers
we are menacing paupers

      crawling with shadows
      shameless with street

our torches scream louder than our lungs,
everything but the world in our eyes

      we will eat our own hearts
          toss the static in the gutters

      no song can make us remember   or forget

our skies are made of steel,
yet they hold nothing in

      without our rage   we have no will to speak

our deaths pass by like flickering gasps of night
      and the flowers are always wilted

          on our graves

Ripening

mother was our curves

      --even her silhouettes were silver

  mother could grow marigolds
     in November

  she was our snake charmer

        (our static cling)

freshman girl

now you can sashay
instead of shuffle

blossom, unfinish
bloom and half-grow

waiting and waiting
to drop your anchor

Little Punk

The wrathful kid with the fierce fingers
and a penchant for torturing ants won't
stop breaking eggs on the sidewalk,
won't respond to the chagrined old lady
shouting from across the street in the
kooky green house with lace for blinds.
He splatters the eggs like a fresh Pollock.
His father works twelve hours a day,
six days a week, in some nearly-extinct
job better left to computers who don't have
two mortgages out on some disfigured dark
eyesore with a leaf-choked lawn and a tornado-
prone roof that blocks out the sunrise.
His mother cleans the kitchen counter
twenty times a day. The trampoline sags
like a heartless sonnet. The basketball net
unthreads in self-pity. *Splat!* Now there are
no more eggs to scramble in silent, screaming testaments, and
the kid heads home for
another sapless sandwich of a supper.

listening for it . . .

. . . the kind of silence
only attics can hear

speechless
and unspeakable

Color-Coded & Iridescent

You dress in dogwood rose,
claret, jungle green;
chisel Chinese violet
out of bones and ebony.

I found a scribbled sonnet
inside your June Bud jeans,
saw the way you danced in Venice,
your lines a sleek, sweet cream.

Your eyes could be a landscape,
its sky every shade of blue.
The instant when your heart stood still:
the most fuchsia part of you.

Softer

I want your sex
the way an engine
grits its teeth

I want your molasses
the way a stock horse
steers the breeze

I want your eloquence
the way a dancer
points her toes

I want your elation
the way a sailboat
becomes the sea

Vilano

On the beach that night,
the wind crawling in shudders
between the dunes,
we sank into the crevices
of raven's eye moonlight
bleeding sonnets on the sand.
We made hasty love in the shallow tide,
the saltwater stinging,
cleaning you out of me,
rushing you into me.

Sometimes, when the ocean freezes,
stunned into undulation,
it remembers our heartbeats,
deeper than a leatherback diving,
with more electricity
than a bluefire jellyfish
defending the sea.

Tide

stubborn white mares
raging up again and again
to feel their foam bodies
flood with grace:

the shore is their mythology

Adulterer

no matter
how many ways
you phrase
the question
his answer
will always be
s*oon*

Bipolar Lexicon

but did you know I drive through scare crows
                pin wings to walls   ladybugs to kites

it's all thunder to my wilderness   and
wilderness inside my thunder

                the startling of your island

      I will take only my goldfish and my gun
            (no suitcase can alleviate *my* tyrants)

I am filled with ghosts and bats and doctored apples
            blowing up cobwebs with cannons

                                you will
find your coins
                inside your footprints

        together we embower beehives
my sinew begs for snails   my bones sigh with aftermath

Addictions

a murderess is on the loose
no asylum could hold her lightning

her beauty so beyond repair,
she will catch fire in the rain

one side of her is a queen
on her way to execution,
unable to believe that nothing can save her:
not her jewels, not her king

the other side does not exist. it is not there anymore

her rage has silenced moonlight,
painted over forests and fathers,
filled the earth with glass and bone

when she smiles,
flowers learn to speak

war swells in the blistering streets,
we bury our dead without bitterness,
promise ourselves that nothing is in vain,
scream and scream in whispers

she laughs herself apart

you will never find her again,
though she will be everywhere

Distance

I allowed you
to sail me over lake beds,
pull me up cliffs,
across broken bridges.
But I could not kiss you
with any trace of thunder,
even when the sun was
sinking into so many oceans.
You told me once
that there would never be
enough sky, but always,
always too many stars.
You wished you could
count them with your heart.
Love was the sacks
of luminous, worthless stones
you made me carry
up and down
blue mountains.

Obstinance

your aberration
is dyslexic and frail,
bats beating at the brink

maniacal mirage
of untapped blue devils
and untested claws

still lamenting the loss of your geometry

you believe in nothing
but Van Gogh's fatal heart

ink into armor into prism into psalm
psalm into sonnet into starling into song

painting true love as an exaltation of larks

Waif

Our voices, ghosts rasping and underfed,
never found, ripening to rot.
Stumbling around on scarred streets, ragged feet.
We go nowhere but tonight.

Prowling sinister alleys
for the bated breaths
that the veiled and protected
have forgotten to take.
We collect them like five-cent cans.

Whispers full of winter
inside the outlines of our doors,
threadbare homeless
stitching ourselves into patterns
so boneless and bare
only damned stars can see the seams.

Our graffiti splashed in sagas
across the bewildered underpass,
our busy tattooed flesh
slashed open vein to vein.

The church bell haunts our hallucination,
a menagerie of psalms bubbling in our veins.

We equate Shakespeare with our greatest loss.
The moon paces the sky
like a worried father,
but not mine.
Not mine.

We were never meant to be saved.

Psych Ward, Fifth Floor

A menagerie of decay, of rabid rot,
of bone and bite and core.
There is no need for venality here,
sneaking cigarettes in our sleep.
Muttering moonstruck beasts,
incurable corpses continue
to wallow and weep.
We clutch the stale screams
in our half-plundered lungs,
and the walls peel and reel
with the frenzy we reek.
The mirrors reflect and reject,
reverse and disconnect.
Good-bye, not good bye,
our hands slip from
cobwebs to grace.
Revolution will come
in a convulsion of violets,
and it will not spare
the deceased.

a ravaged statue

the extinct epic
of her face

endless and endless
with lyric

may be heard
only

in the bones
of balladeers

Grown into the Atmosphere

You had grown into the atmosphere.

I felt your presence
in the invisible morning,
lilies sighing in heaps
on the kitchen table.

I peeled back the air
and blew breath into you,
like the fog that coats the sky in autumn.

Your eyes remained translucent.

Hermit

I have grown a little eccentric,
a little discontent, I suppose,
since I moved my corner rocking chair
to the very center of the den
near the growling, grinning heater
to cover the carpet's bald spot
and began turning the volume to heaven
to drown out the absence of snoring
in the fireplace glow of yellow-orange
and flashing turquoise tongues.

I must admit,
I have also grown
a little unnerved
by the eerie reverie
of snow-silent cats.

A Faith, Rotting

She wore a cross necklace you would
find in a bargain box, the holy rejects
of sacrilegious sales girls, their pearls
undulating, effulgent. She didn't care
that the gold shed itself into a bastard
green, branded and belligerent against
her pale butterfly of a throat. To her,
there was a beautiful irony in the decay
of something so consecrated with
sadness. To her, there was no religion
without the ululation of a mother's
lamentation, rotting into romance,
idolatry in the immaculate inferiority—
a necklace losing sight of heaven faster
than she did the night God weighed
her losses, wrote them into being.

the darkest art

cackling sonnets
inside every snare
spectral sunfalls
beneath roaring hale
unleashing calamity
these most ambrosial
of refrains
rabid moonbeats
become fancy
become flight
bloodless zion
cradled in
precarious constellations
seething grave
of gehenna
beckons with a boil
withered wildflower witches
live on to lament
our wintered woes
sing siren-soft melodies
into blacksmith nights
hearts ablaze
as pillared wax
dripping sonnets
on fir splinters
windows polish into prisms
yawning moonlight
breaking open
in the daze
between black shores
upon perfumed elms

windless waters
still remembered
from the moments
we were faultless
undiminished
in the eyes
of any god

To Whomever Listens Here

I will sustain for you in consecrated constraint,
tethered to this slatted kitchen door.
There are lesser visions, I am certain,
in your more honest reflections of me.

Where will you wait for me
when the yellow dahlias have finished
spinning into dawn?

There are never too many echoes or footfalls between us.

deployed

emily was right about you

from the peril and speck of jade
    in your scrutiny

        (boozer flatfoot, a flair for us floozies)

to the way you yield your demonic seduction
    in the murky, stained, disheveled moments

        (where she and I cannot exist together)

A Single History

we scream into tea
as libertines
walls imploding in our wake

we land our lords
with lethal flair
moon-draped curls
one starlit eagle eye

our threadbare knees
reign victorious

roulette heartbeats
reloading

Mischief

Last Halloween Eve,
you broke my last black heart,
the one sewn to vintage bone.
The graceful tangling
of your breath in the trees
was quite commanding,
the lunacy of your leer so alight.
The jack o' lantern junkie jigsaw sky
spun with helicopters and hellfire,
devils, dastardly delights.
You threatened to take back
the tomboy nights from my reckless veins.
Your candied, treasonous good-bye
melted, unsavored, into the marrow
of my shadow, became the incubus
of every moonrise, the ill-fated starlet
in my soul. We always spoke of speaking
this way. We always believed in
the possibility of morning stars.
But never again will we breathe in
wind-smoked willows side by side,
or even face the delusions of our scars.
The volley of our youth has settled
into the visage of our mystery,
where I will find you
waging wars with your eyes,
forever breaking soapstone angels.

mockings, midnights

the lion wants
what it still has
the warlord cat
it bides its cream
settle this sideshow
sun-starched calloused cleave
merciless minions
spread freelove venom
borneo black plague asps
we report paper cuts
and piranhas
us fragile inner city bees
i didn't hollow
this canyon
between us
i didn't carve it
from a dream
we meet at three ends
romancing embers
into echoes
so many heartbeats
later
you devour
lilac locust breeze
silicone sonnet sundae shade
baskets of billabongs
trapped in your bass
dreaming of frequencies
in the next lane
you never failed
in the phase

you waned
it only matters
when the moon is
unrehearsed
unexplained
electrifying snowflakes
branding bullets
with your everlasting
examining
our apparition
it flies solo
at the seams
shadowing a village
it pebbles
at our feet
we forget
we forgot our every father
somewhere they trace
themselves
back to the tide
somewhere they lose
their opals
in the maze
try try try
we could never
jump-start skies
treason
your lone infatuation
mocking the martyrs
of the blaze
loose chantings
from our fingertips
the only part
of you
i take with me

into coal mines
past the bombs
wherever you flee
i feel your limerick
in my bones
however you undo
i find the starset
in my tree

Relics

memorize me
in the slanted dawn
of your attic,
taking pictures with my heart

unfind me
in the quatrain mist
outside the coffee trees

open up
the farmlit skies
shaking with the sea

lose me
in the newborn dimmet,
unlearn me in your cream

lie stiller
than a peony
bashful in the breeze

shed the solace
wrapped around
the bases of your bones:
autumnal afghans, freesia fleece

put away
those lost engravings
from your father

read to me

the only outcast star
in the tide

strike wilder
than a daisy
dining on its shade

conjure poems
from your sinew,
making all the right mistakes

White Light

the river remembers nothing new

i regret
that i regret nothing

the savages of your solace
the donnybrook you opined
sweep their bitter boiling smoke
up toward the fasting sky

lotus blossoms inherit no meadows

balladry wanes with faithand what fathoms of remorse
haunt the bottom of your heart

no one grieves for harlots
turned to rust
nor weeps for wizards
bespelling dust

fortune-tellers of amour
we weave our astrometry
into stars seen only
from your tower

Interstate, Idle

It cost the moon
and its coterie of stars
to resist your polish
your laurel wither
your celadon stirrings
ripening, undaunted
ripening, because

It took a highway
and its gridlock hysteria
to unleash your eclipse
your fragile granite
your aphotic strikes
darkening, unsparing
darkening, despite

Ode to Anonymous Annulment

nothing more to unearth
by the boroughs of Mexico City
Tolsa bronze, Rufio Tomayo, Reforma Avenue
the onslaught of star-strung shores

shipwrecked in the azure breeze

nothing more to retract
by the thirsty plains of Peru
Colca Canyon, triple-tiered waterfalls
the grape grappa's stinging bite
pottery porn, *Chicha* in the shantytowns

no more to seek
with fuming fever
by the indigenous lace
of erogenous Paraguay

parted paths
along the Pocosol River
exacting Costa Rica's coral kiss

those Ultimate Lights of Havana
rectifying all renunciation

Whitechapel

Mary Jane rang an Irish refrain,
drunk on Ten Bells whiskey.
Her unpolluted apron ablaze,
she surrendered a scarlet shawl
and her weary wildgrass heart
to the rogue incubus cloaked
in the serrated fog, haunting
every step of squalid streets,
preying on its darkest shadows.

She placed the native beauty berries
upon her wooden churchyard grave,
marked with the Unfortunate's brand
she seared upon her own scars
when she abandoned everywhere
that could tie her to anyone.

In the end, there was nothing
she would not do
for a fire.

Suicide Attack

I raised the dead once,
by the handhold of a coma,
beneath the ruin of our grave.

They came stumbling
with their graceless marrow
clamoring from cobwebs,
gasping for the breath
reserved for my last rose.

They sobbed with transient twilight,
choking on severed shadows
from terminal sunsets
and blood-boiling moons.

They asked me, voiceless, waning,
how did I see the sky?

I answered:

in every battling, burning color,
in every flicker of foaming fire
beyond his storming seas.

Cave Art

the runes remembered
this cliff-face charnel house
harboring celibate snakes
feral pirates eroded by waterfalls
a porous pottery tomb
enameled with windows and reflection
arsenical bronze atonement
work-weary malachite odes
paleolithic princes chiseled
and chiding in charcoal
red ochre epochs outlined
with torch marks and eventide
megafauna manganese
bellowings of bison bones
whittled wartimes and reindeer relics
embroidered clashes with the sea
hematite harlots inciting
horseback holocausts
the extinction of aweless echoes
within this null necropolis
within this elegiac eve

Pappaw

He taught himself calligraphy
during his vagabond days
hopping islands and
martyring munitions
hoping to lose himself
in sumptuous, senseless rhythm
amidst the clamoring blazes
and graveyard ghettos,
piles of boulders and bones,
hellish ruptures mauling skies.

Cool-eyed and soundless
in his reeling restraint,
he sketched impetuous ballerinas
in the funereal barracks
parched and poisoned with
the boisterous stench of
reverence, despair, bravura:
a grim carnival of phantoms
peddling peeling sideshows.

Pappaw carved out foxgloves
for smudged sisters in weary pinafores,
handed out bubble gum cigars
to the hollow orphans
drifting in the rubble.
He found denotation in detonation,
regalia in the skeletal regime
staggering in haggard conquest,
ascendency etched into the echoes
they left behind to atone for

their sacrilegious tempests,
gray infidel snow.

A Distant Relation

dexter ain't no butterfly
hacking open baby lizards
in the craggy kansas sun
taking ole tammy lynn
for hair-trigger spins in the
flowing molten cornfields
his granddaddy abandoned
to narcoleptic scarecrows
wallowing in wireworms
five or six cyclones ago

Asylum Patient 141

Corruption corrodes
the most uncertain of us,
rusts the very bones of saints.
It steals the fractured heart of science,
filters it into fairy tales,
forensic fables, reluctant lullabies.

We romanticize our demons
in this frenzied, fetid freeze,
this place of Cimmerian shade
and unadorned obscurity.
We play both violence and victim,
as they falter hand in hand.

Here, we are anonymous
in our absolution,
riotous with remorseless misery,
teasing stifled screams into
black winters, yawning stars.

Our malignant veins flow with rabid venom;
our hearts retain the incineration of the sun.

They confiscate our secret languages,
our apple seeds,
our potential for potency.

In here, we forget
the calamity of our daughters,
the sageness and solidity
of our mothers,

every cursory gaze of adoration
from grandfathers,
every mountain moved
by the brothers in silhouette
we memorized long ago.

We unleash our cheerless skies,
repel our distant thunder.
To absolve ourselves of stigma,
we accept thoughtful torture,
barbaric battery.
Contrition is a price
we cannot afford to pay.

There are damnable stones
we cannot unthrow,
now that our mirrors
have imploded,
now that our walls
have been razed
to righteous earth.

We locked away our maladies,
relishing our ragged wounds.
Now we dance for no one
but the mirage of moon peering
through barred immunity.

After the unknowing
comes the sequined ballroom haze.
After the unbecoming
comes the boundless beaming Bellatrix
warring with Polaris
up in the seasick night.

Wednesday Night on the Ward

you listen to them
rave and riot and rehearse
long enough
you start to sprout wings
take flight
inside your own sedated hell
you begin to repine
all of the footholds
you chose to omit
not so very long ago
the distinctions
escorting you to the gallows
when you were smoother
and more wondrous
illusion still glazing your enamel eyes
in your cousin's attic
channeling saffron and cedar
we opened fire
against the lemon-scoured walls
atop a quilt fussy with foxgloves
forever shed to should have never
the altitude of a scalawag star
when they snatch the lights
the nurses haunt the doors
imposed unspecifics
whitewashed in the bowels
of the disenchanted tower
where i first wounded my mother
where I whispered good-bye
too late once again
to my well-founded father

two disfigured decades later
too intemperate to contemplate
his silently roaring absence
until it struck me like a startled viper
inside a coward's waking dream
leaving me with rotting ambition
a mummified marriage
strung out on the spinning night
a powerless undoing in my belly
unwinding me into the warring sea
ships collide inside my heart
I have been here before
in this defiled unmarked cell
in this perfectly-polished prison
wielding unspoken weapons
where they shuffle us
into conga lines, resuscitations, recitations
I will swim continents and car lengths and cataclysms away
we embrace the embroidery
of our grandest wild gardens
calendula spice, canterbury bells, pink-bellied anemone
the ones we water only
in the momentary moonlight
when the winter branches
are free of opulence
for once unencumbered
by nature's every last
daredevil whim

Now Lucid

What we took from each other
were not counterblows,
but inspiration and blue fire.
Diamonds line our memories
like sizzling constellations.
There will be no more of our
bareback alleyway love,
raw scars ripped open
on rippled shoulders,
mutiny in our mutuality.
We forge the illusions
of our idols, chant to gods
of earth, lust, lions, wars.
There are no more calamities
to weather our shivering nights,
no more bee stings to relish.
If we suffer at all,
we suffer in phantasms, chimeras,
paling next to statues.
If sedition ever spread
its incestuous seed
into the trenches
of our feral gardens,
our tatter would never
traverse the war.
Our malice melts history,
boasts itself in buoyant headlines
forged of burning gold.
We shallow our heartbeats
with gaudy show tunes
and campfire ghosts

from the embers
of childhood convolution.
We steady our heartbeats
with the whispers
of our grandmothers,
breathing endless farewells
through stubborn vintage phones.

Farewell to Seafaring

And then no more wagers
lost to shimmering foreign waters,
no more golden doll-faced doxies
clad in spicy salsa dresses
stalking the salty, stale sailors
straggling in from every one
of the seven surly seas.

We survived the cannons
raging just beyond the coral,
the vast plush of violet sky
beating with fresh-born stars.

We were dazzled by the
smoking aurulent sunsets
and spectral black whales
thunderous in their massive grace,
exonerated by the quarter-moon,
enraptured by the soul of Belisama,
goddess of fire and crashing lights.

Carpeted in sonnet-sewn mist
and twilight-netted awnings
we watched the ruthless sunrise
execute preemptive constellations
memorized every transient tomorrow.

Green River Eulogy

don't search for me on neon streets
don't long for me come christmas eve
just think of soaring honey trees
drifting in the spangled breeze
and you will hear that where i go
has no more rules to ebb or slow
the embers i once called my heart
now a matchstick in the dark

Five Mornings Later

these parking lot ghosts listen well,
silencing their silencing
against the frigid embryo of dawn
obscuring the delirious shuffle of
tenuous scars and evanescent sedans
overtaking the dreamless diameter
created in covert, insidious corners
where the faintly-faring congregate
in rummaging distressed quartets
to pillage streetlight and camaraderie
to speak in bloodless languages
escalating from quick to marrow
freeing swaying, cryptic melodies
we must, we must remember fondly
the pillars now powdering between us
gangrene granite withering with atrophy
they foretold this farewell in chamomile
you never rest your speculation on me
you never touch your finger to my trembling

Brothers

I pieced together mine
out of heirloom anecdotes
and alien bits of familial folklore
from the trenches of a childhood
bristling with rickety shadows
erratic and fitful, existing in
the garish borderline where
I stored all my barbed angles
in kitschy boxes. He once healed
a disarmed duckling, unleashed
titanic plodding tortoises
into our shaggy gray yard
adorned with weeping willows
spilling woe into the prodigal soil
poisoning azaleas. He stood over me
in every sandbox, commanding
the construction of castles,
his tenacious shade shrouding all reverie.
He was tyrannical at losing or winning,
his bike was gray, gleamed with gloating.
He conditioned the other cul-de-sac cherubs
to toss pebbles at my head because
I would always somehow deserve it.
Now he scowls through every Easter,
sighs resignedly under his breath
at the anemic table littered
with the dregs
of our lifeless inheritance.
He checks the wall clock
above the white brick fireplace
in the pitted den

every time our mother speaks.
He asks me nothing,
I ask for nothing,
matching mazarine eyes
never failing to
incite insinuation.

The Ones Before Ours

Crazed as cobras they were,
purging venom in the hollow dust.
They came hunting sovereigns,
more indulgent gods, a hotbed
heaven devoid of all restraint,
finding bygone littered bones
blistering in flimsy haystacks.

But who were we to disenchant
their impassioned appellations,
to reduce their brazen testament
to indigenous residue?
We found carvings of infants
and infernos and idols lost to
the chronology of salvation,
cryptic sagas of spontaneous courage,
romance brimming in the stones.

They claw our crowing windows
when the half-moon is sizzling,
carnal excision still burning in
their shivering nomadic bones.

Mapping

we finished in frigid calligraphy
what we never felt the need to do
heart to heart
fire to frenzy to fracture
there were vast, luscious moments
we will remember in
agave Antigua whispers
Bavarian bread crumbs
winter-capped Norse summits
bleeding blue lyrics on Baltic beaches
crawling through granite and Greenland
deflowering Irish violet lullabies and
English rose sonnets in our shrieking wake
you manifested the anonymous almond shores
where I will one day overture my soul
these posturing postcards
will be our postscripts
those Nova Scotia steamship whitetips
our final coup de grâce

Acknowledgments

Digital Americana, Fall 2012
"Addictions"
"Distance"

4 and 20, January 2013
"listening for it . . ."

The Rathalla Review, Fall 2013
"Without Poetry"

Midnight Circus, Fall 2013
"Degenerating" (short story)

Hello Horror, Halloween Issue, 2013
"Psych Ward, Fifth Floor"

Deep South Magazine, April 2014
"Little Punk"
"A Faith, Rotting"

Broad!, Mother's Day Issue, 2014
"Ripening"

Black Heart Magazine, May 2014
"Waif"
"Obstinance"
"Vilano"

Obsessed With Pipework, Spring 2014
"Color-Coded & Iridescent"
"Softer"

Dark Moon Digest, October 2014
"Beige" (short story)

Skidrow Penthouse, December 2014
"Without It" (reprint)

The Belleville Park Pages, January 2015
"Bipolar Lexicon"

Belle Reve, March 2015
"Tide"
"Grown Into the Atmosphere"
"Addictions" *(reprint)*
"Distance" *(reprint)*
"Snow White"

The Bitchin' Kitsch, April 2015
"Hermit"

Rat's Ass Review, September 2016
"freshman girl"
"A Single History"

Better Than Starbucks, October 2016
"Mischief"

The Front Porch Review, October 2016
"Addictions" (reprint)

Sick Lit Magazine, February 2017
"Relics"
"Mapping"
"the darkest art"
"mockings, midnights"
"deployed"
"To Whomever Listens Here"
"Distance" (reprint)
"Little Punk" (reprint)
"Color-Coded & Iridescent" (reprint)
"Ripening" (reprint)

The Scarlet Leaf Review, May 2017
"Pappaw"
"Brothers"
"Five Mornings Later"
"The Ones Before Ours"
"Asylum Patient 141"

The Dying Dahlia Review, Summer 2017
"Adulterer"
"a ravaged statue"

Jersey Devil Press, Special Victorian Mash-Up Issue, August 2017
"Whitechapel"

Down in the Dirt, January 2018
"Farewell to Seafaring"

Quail Bell, January 2018
"A Faith, Rotting" (reprint)

Danse Macabre, January 2018
"Addictions" (reprint)

Harbinger Asylum, March 2018
"Without Poetry" (reprint)

Poehemian, March 2018
"Relics" (reprint)

Firefly, March 2018
"listening for it…" (reprint)

The Wax Paper, April 2018
"Hermit" (reprint)
"Little Punk" (reprint)

Clockwise Cat, May 2018
"the darkest art" (reprint)

Rhetoric Askew, June 2018
"Color-Coded & Iridescent" (reprint)
"Ode to Anonymous Annulment" (reprint)
"Pappaw" (reprint)

Pacific Poetry, November 2018
"Obstinance" (reprint)
"Suicide Attack" (reprint)

For the Sonorous, 2018

"A Faith, Rotting" (reprint)

About the Author

Megan Denese Mealor has been creating stories, characters, and poems since her first set of crayons. Language has been her torch, confidant, and conduit throughout the vast surreal maze of mental illness that has permeated her childhood and adolescence, relentlessly stalking her into adulthood. Diagnosed with bipolar disorder at fifteen, Megan has battled to survive the harrowing vacillation of mania, depression, and spiritual numbness of the illness's onslaught, as well as the heartbreaking destruction it has wrought upon every faucet of her life. Much of her writing was created in psychiatric wards while recovering from bone-weary breakdowns. Ironically, most were written with crayons (if Megan cannot find the humor in these things, then she has learned nothing).

Megan was born and bred in Jacksonville, Florida, a land of neon bridges and bustling heart. She lives with her partner Tony, their four-year-old son Jesse, and two ancient mollycoddled cats JubJub and Trigger. Megan's hobbies include alligators, bowling, calligraphy, gardening, beachcombing, air hockey, history, photography, beadwork, yoga, and ghost hunting.

About the Press

Unsolicited Press is a small press in Portland, Oregon. Founded in 2012, the team strives to publish exemplary poetry, creative nonfiction, and fiction. Learn more at www.unsolicitedpress.com.

www.ingramcontent.com/pod-product-compliance
Lightning Source LLC
Chambersburg PA
CBHW052104110526
44591CB00013B/2347